First published by Parragon in 2012

Parragon
Chartist House
15–17 Trim Street
Bath BA1 1HA, UK
www.parragon.com

Written by Annie Baker
Illustrated by Barroux
Edited by Laura Baker
Designed by Ailsa Cullen
Production by Jonathan Wakeham

ISBN 978-1-78186-747-1

Printed in China

I LOVE YOU WHEN ...

PaRragon

Bath • New York • Singapore • Hong Kong • Cologne • Delhi
Melbourne • Amsterdam • Johannesburg • Shenzhen

I love you when you're being funny.

I love you when it's wet outside.

I love you when you want to hide.

I love you when it's very breezy!

I even love you when you're sneezy.

I love you when we rush to and fro,

and I love you when there's nowhere to go.

I love you when you're feeling sleepy.

I love you when you're sad and weepy.

I love you when you giggle ...

when you wiggle ...

when you wriggle ...

I love you when you're snuggly.

I love you when you're huggly.

I love you when you say, "I love you, too."

But mostly, I love you whenever
I'm with you.

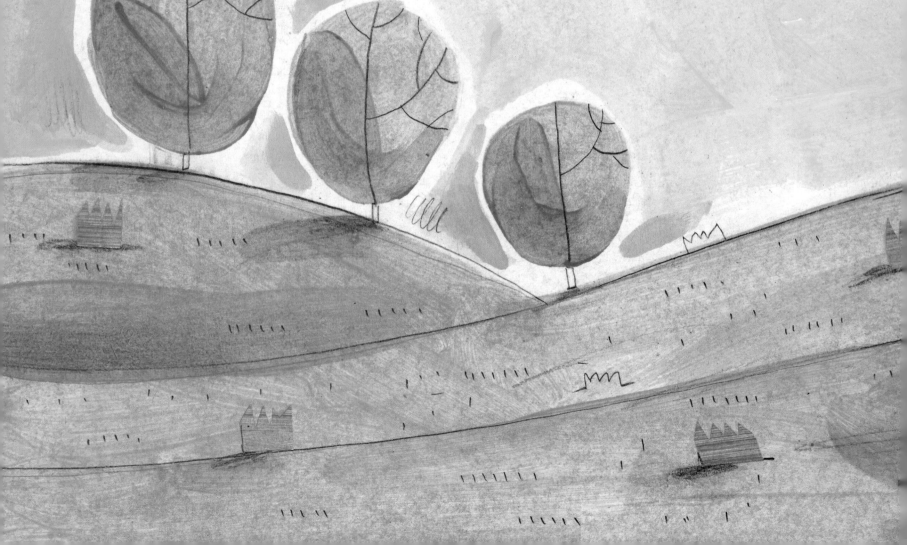

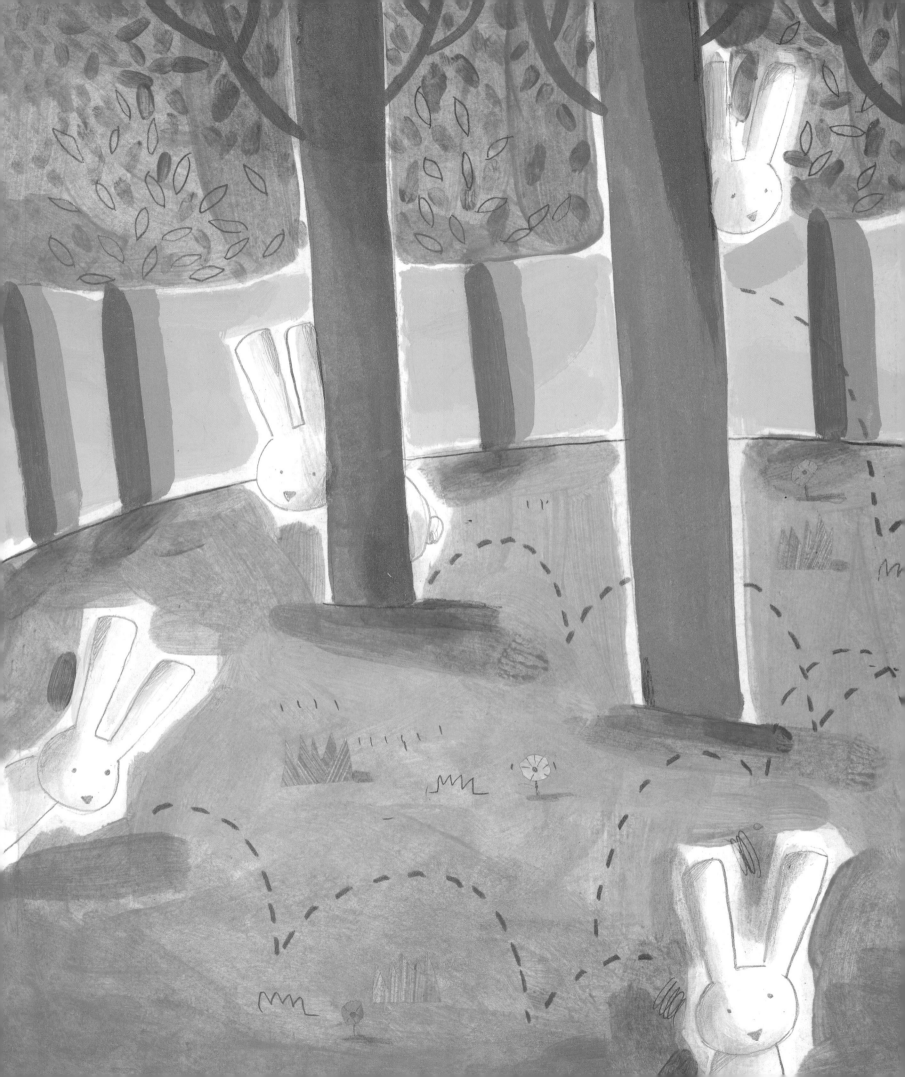